PLEASE,

When Corinne Aldis, producer of BBC Radio Leicester's programme "Morning Extra", ran a competition and asked local children to write prayers on various subjects, she was happily surprised when the prayers came in – surprised at their number, at the skill of the illustrations, and at the feelings they all expressed.

Although for reasons of space we can include only a small selection of the prayers and drawings, we are grateful to everyone who contributed. The royalties from this book will go to help other, less fortunate, children, in Leicester through COPE, and on a broader level through Cancer Relief Macmillan Fund.

Donna Hancock

Royalties from the sale of this book will be divided between
COPE and Cancer Relief Macmillan Fund.

If anyone wishes to know more about their work,
or to send a donation, their addresses are:

COPE
Arlen House
Salisbury Road
Leicester
LE1 7QS

Cancer Relief Macmillan Fund
Anchor House
15–19 Britten Street
London
SW3 3TZ

please God...

BBC Radio Leicester's Book of Children's Prayers

Compiled by
Carol Watson

Collins: Fount Paperbacks

First published in Great Britain
by Fount Paperbacks, London in 1989

Copyright © 1989
BBC Radio Leicester

Printed and bound in Great Britain by
William Collins Sons & Co. Ltd, Glasgow

FOREWORD

I first came into contact with COPE through the five-year-old twins Kit and Laura Moore. I met them at the Children of Courage Award service at Westminster Abbey in December 1988. I was there to read the citations of bravery for the children being presented to H.R.H. The Duchess of York, and young Kit was one of these children. He had been honoured for supporting his twin sister Laura in her two-and-a-half year fight agains leukaemia, and for bravely donating his own bone marrow when she relapsed with the disease.

Over a special lunch for the children at the House of Lords following the presentation ceremony Harry and Gail, the twins' parents, confided in me that only the previous evening they had been informed that although the transplant had been a success, the disease had returned to Laura and she now had only a few weeks to live. No one else at the award ceremony was aware of this, save a few members of the *Woman's Own* staff who had agreed to keep it to themselves. Personally I will never forget Laura's face that day, her dark eyes showing all the premature maturity that comes with great suffering. It will be with me always.

Harry and Gail had spent many months camped on the children's ward at the Leicester Royal Infirmary over the past years, in order to give Laura 24-hour parental care. They saw first-hand some of the difficulties of caring for children with leukemia and cancer on an open ward. The treatment causes loss of immunity to infection. The children, therefore, are at risk from cross infection from other patients.

When Laura was eventually placed in the new purpose-built adult bone marrow transplant unit, they realized what sort of facilities could be made available for children. They also realized that having the technology to administer chemotherapy and radiotherapy, and to perform bone marrow transplants was only the tip of the iceberg, for these things had to take place in the right environment, with adequate facilities and properly trained staff. COPE sets out to provide this environment through the building of a dedicated treatment centre at the Leicester Royal Infirmary. In addition, it will introduce community nurses for children with cancer, and COPE-CARE nurses. The project has the full backing of Leicestershire Health Authority.

Sadly, little Laura died on 28th January 1989 – just thirty-two days after I met her. Her death was a tragedy, but it was not a waste. Out of her short life came the inspiration behind the project that will help a lot more children like her. I could do no better than end by quoting a few lines from a prayer specially written by her daddy, and included in this anthology. It expresses the things she really cared for –

> *We thank you for her life, the joy it brought and the privilege of sharing it. Seek out the beauty in our lives, dear Christ, that we may perpetuate her ways, her name and aspirations, that the humble might be great, the dark be turned to light and the sick be cared for.*

ANTHONY ANDREWS

Laura Jane Moore

Born 7th November 1983
Died Saturday, 28th January 1989

Her life was short, but so is that of all the brightest flowers. She accomplished such a lot in oh so short a life span. Her battle against Leukaemia encouraged many parents and children. The story of her relapse, the fight back and donation of "good soldiers" from twin brother Kit to fight the "bad soldiers" in her bone marrow was the heartwarming story of the year. Her calm but resolute acceptance of the fight was the real inspiration behind COPE. She was thus its true creator. She also took the family to London, where Kit received the Children of Courage Award from the Duchess of York, on the very steps in Westminster Abbey where the Kings and Queens of England have been crowned for the past 700 years.

However, her life was not only associated with disease. It was mainly one of joy and light, pleasure in her native countryside and being with her family. Perhaps the culmination of her short life was to accomplish Prep. school and for her and Kit to take the parts of Mary and Joseph in the school nativity play.

She loved colour, and this was epitomised by a fondness for rainbows, hence her love of the Care Bear stories.

One day, shortly before her death, whilst driving over the Pennine hills, she saw the most complete and beautiful rainbow she had ever seen. The happiness and delight in her face captured in that moment mirrored the spectrum of colours she saw. If a rainbow could bring her such happiness then, surely, rainbows must form the stairway to paradise. So, please whenever you see a rainbow, remember Laura.

INTRODUCTION TO COPE

COPE stands for the Children's Oncology Unit Appeal, an appeal for a children's cancer unit at the Leicester Royal Infirmary, specifically for the treatment of malignant diseases such as leukaemia and cancer. As the treatment can be distressing, and can lead to a loss of immunity to infection, COPE aims to set up a separate unit at the Leicester Royal Infirmary where the children will have a better environment in which to overcome their illness.

One child who lost her battle against disease but who was the inspiration behind COPE was Laura Jane Moore, whose story is told earlier.

A Prayer for Laura

Almighty God, take Laura into your care. Enfold her with your love and let her now know freedom from sickness and pain. May she walk in your light in peace and tranquility through the pathways of your eternal Kingdom and may she know everlasting salvation.

We thank you for her life, the joy it brought and the privilege of sharing it. Seek out the beauty in our lives, dear Christ, that we may perpetuate her ways, her name and aspirations, that the humble might be great, the dark be turned to light and the sick be cared for.

Grant us grace, dear Lord, to hold her in our love until that day when, on another shore and in a greater light, we may see more than puzzling reflections in the mirror and our knowledge shall no longer be partial but whole, like God's knowledge of us, and we may live once again together in unity.

CANCER RELIEF
MACMILLAN FUND

Cancer Relief Macmillan Fund is a national charity working to help improve the quality of life for people with cancer, and their families. It was founded in 1911 by Douglas Macmillan.

Today, Cancer Relief Macmillan Fund is perhaps best known for providing Macmillan nurses, of which there are now over 600 in the UK. Cancer Relief also helps through grants to people with cancer; builds Macmillan units for in-patient and day care; funds a medical and nursing education programme; and supports four Associated Charities which provide information about cancer and support to people affected by it.

CONTENTS

Sorry,

Lord ...

SORRY.

Sorry lord for all the wars
Sorry for starvation
make our world kind and caring
and let no one suffer.
Sorry lord for, violence, please.
make our world kind like yours.
Let this world be like heaven
and sorry for what I've done wrong
Thank you.

AMEN

JAYMINI PATEL

Please Jesus
Pleasehelp us to
Say Sorry when
We have done

something   wrong.

Amen.

Jonathan Wdd

Dear
    Lord
        I'm so sorry. I have been
Mean and jealous over the past week
to my brother and it's his birthday. I'll
try to be kind towards him now that
he is eight years old.

        Amen.

            Age 11.   Gaggan Dhaliwal.

Forgiveness Prayer

Oh Lord forgive,
For we do not love,
Our neighbours like we should.
We hurt each other,
and we do not care,
for anyone except ourselves.
I look around the world,
and all I can see
is pain, and hurt, and suffering.
So in this prayer,
I beg you forgiveness,
for everyone around the world.

Amen.

by Paul M.

Sorry God for upseting my

Dad and mum and I'll be

greatfull for whot Ive

got and Ill never be greedy

and be like a hooly goon

at football matchs

Aramen

Andrew

sorry god for the cruel
things I have done especially yesterday
when I was playing and a dog with
no home came up to me and started
to lick my hand and all my friends
were looking so I kicked the dog
just to be big, Please god I am
sorry. I should of stroked the dog
and try to give it a home
sorry god.

The End

by

Leon Kirby

age 11

a true story

Sorry God for what ever I have
        done
For being mean to others and
not helping those who are in
        need
For blaming others for what
they havern't done.

Being mean to my family and
friends because I am going
through a rough patch
In Jesus name I pray

        Amen

        By Punam
            Lakhani

        Age 10

Through the eye of an addict

Dear God

Sorry there's not a better
way to say this but in a
way I'm happy to be
alive but sometime's I
don't think so because no body
understands me. God I'm so afraid
you see I've never told any one this
but I take drugs I'm so sorry
really I am, please forgive
me

Amen

Dear God,

 We're very sorry that we are not doing what you ask. But _most_ of us try our best. We're sorry for the changes we bring into this world. We're also sorry for the bad things we say about you. Sorry God.

AMen
x

JOEDIE BRADGATE

Sorry Lord,
        For all the things I
have done wrong during the past
week. I have been bad-tempered
and nasty towards my family and
friends and I feel very guilty
for the way I have treated
them. I should have known
better and shouldn't have taken
it out of them.
                Please forgive me,

By Joanne Douglas-Boyd 4r
        and Sixnwir Griag 4r.

by Kelly Astill age 10

Dear Lord,

Forgive me for those things that I have done wrong today.

I try very hard to not argue and I try to understand other peoples' points of view but sometimes I can't help losing my temper.

The stupidest things annoy me, I find it so hard to say sorry and to mean it.

Please help me to be more understanding,
Amen

Charlotte Collier & Lettie Bishop

Forgive us for......
losing our temper with our friends and relations.
saying things that are hurtful.
Lieing
saying things behind other peoples backs
that we don't mean.
being spiteful
not helping others.
We will try not to do the above.

Amen.

By T. Walker and A. Dunstan.

by Lucy
Phillips age 10

Thank you,
God . . .

Dear God

Thank You for

caring about us

and loving us

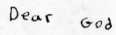

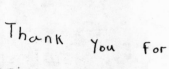

From

April

Dear God
        I like the way yuo made
the earth and the animals
a the sun
and the otherplanets.
Thankyuo for everything.

Jonathan

by Daniel Green
    age 10

Thanks for the rabbit
that hops and Jumps.
And thanks for the camel
that has two humps.
Thank-you for hockey
and games we play,
And thank-you for people
Who help me each day.

Tony Davis Aged 12

Dear God

Thank you for electricity and thank you for our house and garden and thank you for the farm animals and our animals too and thank you for our cars and our street and our class and clothes and school and thank you for our body and machines and thank you for the world and Mum and Dad and thank you for fish and the rain and rainbows and thank you for the roads and the air and thank you for my life.

Amen

by Claire Atkinson
age 6

A Thank you Prayer
        Peter Townsend 11 years

Dear God   Thank you for our families and, our friends.
Thank you for plants and, ~~an~~ animals and, especially
our pets. Thanks for the Ozone layer that
protects our Earth although we are not looking after it.
Thanks fors the farms and, the countries that
suply our food.
            A men

HANKS

Thank you for inventors who made wheelchairs and tricycles and walking frames and cars. Thank you for people who look after our chairs and for physios who help us to use our strength. Thank you for making Tony and Andrew my friends.

Andrew   Chris   Tony

Christopher Rock   Aged 11

Dear Father God
Thank you for the World.
the beautiful Trees and
Flowers and Favourite
things like tractors
and my favourite tractor
the JCB but for the
animals as well
                    Amen
         Richard Bark Age 7

Robert Wallace
Age 10

THANK YOU LORD

Thank you lord for the world and sea.
Thank you lord for the sun and moon.
Thank you lord for the birds and animals.
Thank you lord for the friends and families.
Thank you lord for the earth.
Thank you lord for the trees and mountains.
    Thank you lord for everything.

by Jitendra
    Chouhan
        age 13¾

Dear
 God

Thankyou for
friends and family

thankyou for
the teacher that
helps us all through
the year thankyou
for the poeple that
help us thankyou that
we have you
              Amen

                    by Kelly
                    Parr

ThankYou Lord for all Your help.
You help me as much as You
can when I am ill and I
appreciate it dearly. I Love
to walk in The country Where I
Live. Oh! I am so Lucky to
Live in the country. Amen.

Freya Tyers 8 Years

by Katherine Denton
age 7

Dear Jesus
Thank you for
the birds and the
dogs and the weter
that we drink
Thank you for the food
we eat
and our dinner.
Ladies who cook
our   dinner

Amen.

annaMarieLinney

pleas god stop   The famin
pleas god stop   The fiting
in The wold
Thanks goD for making my dog
beter when it brock its leg
Thakes for Heping my guandcd
get ofer his hart atack.
Thanks   lord for my frends
my home   and animals
Thanks lord for school shop
and JObes.

by John mayner

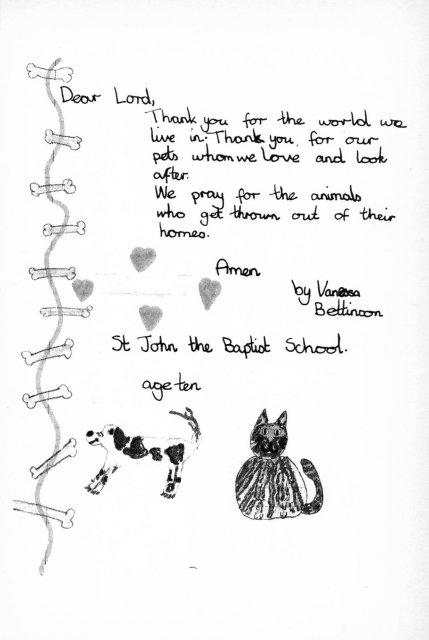

Dear Lord,
Thank you for the world we
live in. Thank you, for our
pets whom we love and look
after.
We pray for the animals
who get thrown out of their
homes.

Amen

by Vanessa
Bettinson

St John the Baptist School.

age ten

for food.

Thank you Lord For Food
For Potatos Baked Hot in the oven
and For Fish From the Chip Shop
For Strawberry Ice Cream on suny
days. Thank you For My fravarate Chocolate
chunchie TOFFe.

David
Allun
Age 13

by Benjamin
Pound
age 9

by Carley Clark
age 10

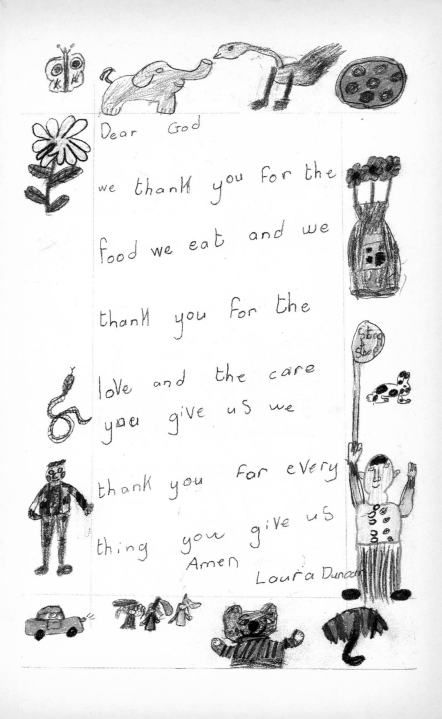

Dear God

we thank you for the

food we eat and we

thank you for the

love and the care
you give us we

thank you for every

thing you give us
Amen

Laura Duncan

Dear god

Thankyou for all the good food we eats. Help those who have no food

A MEN

name   Bhavin Barmar
shoool   St Johns the Baptist   Shcool
Aeg Age   9

John Reeves, 11 years old
A prayer for thanksgiving.

Dear God
thankyou for the food you give us and the plants that grow the food for us, thankyou for the water we can drink, thankyou for cows and goats that gives us milk, but could you give the poor people in the world some rain so they can have clean water and corn, fruits, rice and some money for machines that can help them not to die by infections from insects please. would you please let this happen.

Amen.

Tommorow.

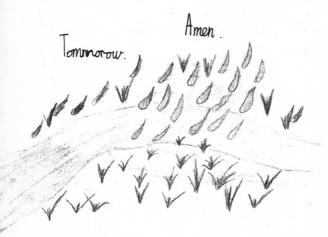

Today.

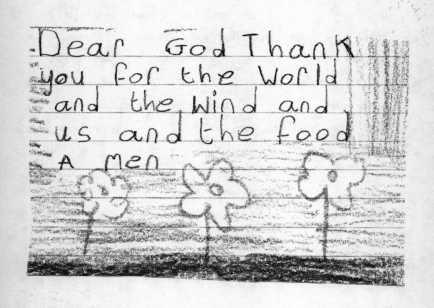

Dear God Thank
you for the World
and the Wind and
us and the food
A men

michael J Weaver

Dear Lord

Thank you for all the Food that comes
from the countries in the world.

Steven knox 10 years

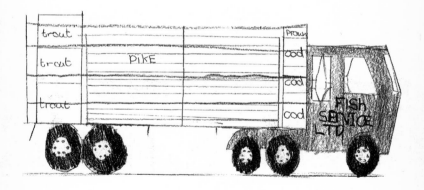

for families and friends

Thank you, God, for our
families and friends;
For mums, for dads
and brothers and sisters,
as well as grandparents.
Without them we would
be lonely.
We also would not get
toys or holidays.
In fact, life would be awful.
So thank you a lot
for families.

Amen   Alexander Chick

by Amanda
Brown
age 10

Dear God

Thank you for my school
Thank your for my friends
Friends make me happy
My Mum is kind
She cooks samosas
Anwar is my brother
He talks to me.
Nasira is my sister
She makes me clothes
Thank you for my famiy
They make me very happy

Basira Siddiq

Dear God.

Thank you for our friends and familys. Help us share our friends with people who have not got any friends. Thank you for our friends that we play with. Help

the people that are old Thank you for our mums and dads and brothers and sisters who care for us

In Jusus name
Amen

Sandeep Hothi

Dear God thank you for
my house, my bike and my
food. Please make my
grandmas rumatisam
get better and make
her have a nice time
in Canada.
                Sasrikalji

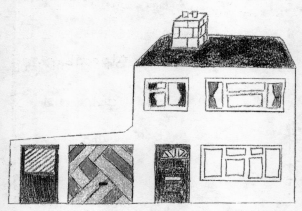

by michael Bradbury age 11

Thank you Lord for giving me such
a great family and my friends.
    Thank you for being next to me
and giving me a nother brother
after my first brother died
Thank you Lord for everything you've
do for me and my family
        Amen

            by Alpa Sharma

please god
can my mum and Dad
live to go to Heavean
and god bless
my baby consien
And my Grand parants
thank you for my life
Hymen

Robert butler 4in

by
Emma Patterson
age 7

Dear Lord

I pray for my family and friends

for their health and happiness.

Give them strength to make right

decisions in a world
full of
temptations

Amen

Julia Booth

i

... for

animals

Lee Morris
age 7 (nearly)

Dear God thank you
for all the animals
help all the RSPCA
people in their work

Thank you God for
looking after my
pets and my gerbil
It is ill and
my gerbils are tow
girls. but one is
called Gordon and
one is
called Glenda.

by
Nicola
Staley

Dear Father,

   Thank you for the world you made
and all the creatures and birds.
Help the animals the that are dying out.
Stop people killing animals for their skins.
Help us Lord to look after them
                    Amen

Jeremy Bickerstaffe

Age 10

Seal

by Amy Williamson
age 10

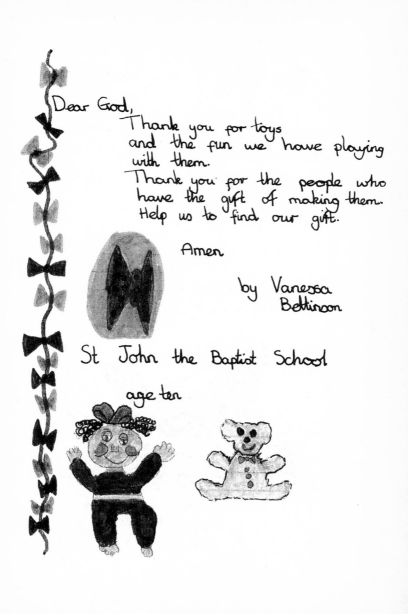

Dear God,
Thank you for toys
and the fun we have playing
with them.
Thank you for the people who
have the gift of making them.
Help us to find our gift.

Amen

by Vanessa
Bettinson

St John the Baptist School

age ten

DearGOD thank you fo
inthe world. <u>Please</u>
that Steal
the male and
wont have
veryupset

A men

Thomas

all the birds

stop all the people
the eggs, because
Females birds
any babies and will be

oxford-Smith
Age 7

Thank you God for pets. thankyou

for the animals that have soft

and fluffy fur. thankyou for the

people like the RSPCA and the

vet who help animals thankyou

for our School pet Sooty. I

like Sooty Amen

by Hazel
Richardson
age 7

Thank   you   God   for   teaching   people   to   help   animals   When   thay   are   ill   or   hurt   thank   you   God   for   all   the   things   thay   eat   thank   you   God   for   my   cat   tigger   amen

by Matthew shaw age 7

Thank you God for rabbits and
guinea pigs and hamster and all
the others
a pet I pets. I wish I had
        I Love pets.

Jody Toon
Age 6

Dear God please Help Me Find My
next door neighbours cat please do
because he was only a kitten
and I liked him so much His name was
Lucky and no one else wanted
him Amen

by Kerry Taylor   Age 7 (nearly)

Dear Lord,

Thank-you very much for the animals that live in our world. May you help the whale killers and other people hunting animals to realize that if they carry on killing the endangered species these will become extinct. May we also remember not to demolish animals' homes. Thank-you Lord.

Amen.

By Natalie Abbott

St. John the Baptist School.
Age ten

Animal rights

Thank-you for all the animals in todays world

I think it is wrong to hurt

It is their nature for foxes to kill and

other animals to kill them.

However for man's pleasure

I think it is wrong

We need to help keep the

Wildlife safe.

       Amen

             Jessica Chasity (11 years)

Thank you god For making us look
AFter our pets and carering For
Them Thank you For teaching us
to take Them to The vets when
They are Ill

A men

by Laura Hart
Age 6

thank you god for my pet
tortoise and the things I have
to feed it and thank god
for all the Animals and all
the things they eat we
thank you for looking after
them we thank you god
for the things they drink
and for loveing them and
careing for them too and the
the bed they sleep in at
night for ever and ever amen
by Andrew Cowperthwaite
Age 7

A Prayer to Say Please

Dear Jesus, Help
all the People who

are being nasty to
other People
and animals. Please help
them to became
Kinder

Amen

Steven
Blackwell Age 7

Please
God ...

Dear God,
          Please could you make laurie my
dad well again for I would so
like to see him walk for the
first time in my life.
I sorry for answering my mum
back and for upsetting her when
I'm naughty.

                    Rebecca Jackson

Shirley Musson, aged 11

I am sad Lord, for people stare at me
in the street. I am just like other
people except that my body needs a
wheelchair. Please help other people
to be more understanding and help
me to keep smiling.

Dear God, Please help me
to forgive my friend. Give
me the courage to confront
her. We had an argument
over a boy and I don't
know what to do. She's
the best friend I've ever
had and I don't want
to loose her over something
silly. I really miss having
her around and I'm really
lonely. Please God, Please.

                    Amen

By Debbie Roberts (14) and Emma Tildesley (14)

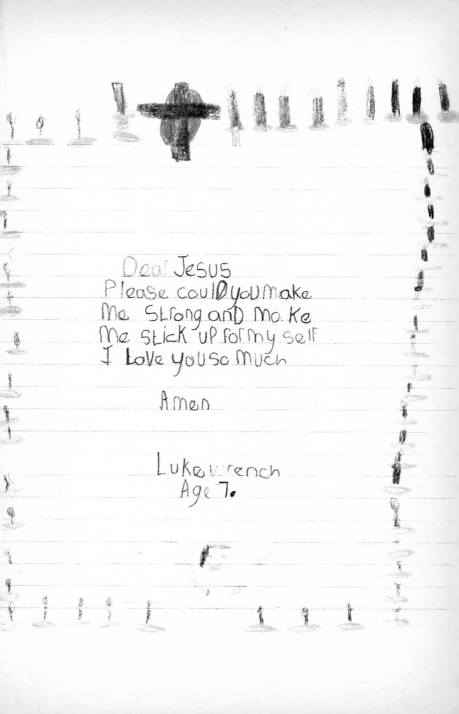

Dear Jesus
Please could you make
me strong and make
me stick up for my self
I love you so much

Amen

Luke Wrench
Age 7.

Please God can you help me
With my Maths and please
help me te be good and
please help me to be quiet.

Jonathan Hugo Piggin Age 9

Georgina Taylor   10 years

A famly and friends prayer

Dear God

Please help all the people whos
families were hurt in the tragedy
football match and help those who
are suffering. help us to be kinder
to our friends and to help our
friends too, in something they can
not do.

Help us Lord

Amen.

Lord

Please let it rain for people in

Sudan and not to let it rain too

Much so it floods.

In Jesus Name We Pray

Amen

BY Gavin Dexter age 11

Please Jesus

Help the people who have not
got a home to go to, when it is cold and
the people who not have got anything to eat.

A Men.

Parry Randles. 9

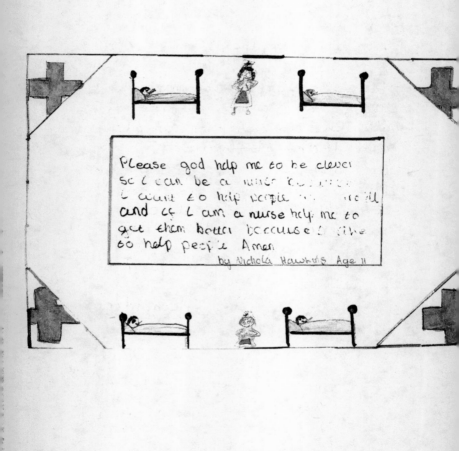

Please god help me to be clever
so I can be a nurse because
I want to help people ......
and if I am a nurse help me to
get them better because I like
to help people Amen
by Nichola Hawkins Age 11

Please God help me, to
help my cousin whose ill
at the moment. What
can I do to help him
or others in his situation.
Please God give me the
strength to help others
in need.
    Amen.

                    Harninder
                        Rai.

Dear god, I won't be sitting here for long and nattering away, and I also don't do this often (as you know). So I hope you can just understand my feelings. For the past week my friends have broken up with me. They have not told me why and what I have done. They won't even talk properly to me. So I am really upset and asking this once in my life if you could help me out. I know you have other better things to do than listen to me so I will leave it to you. But please please help me.

<u>Seema Kainth</u> (14)

Plesee O God When I go across the
thanel on my holiday be with me and
make it a safe journey all the way
for me and my famley,

MZ.

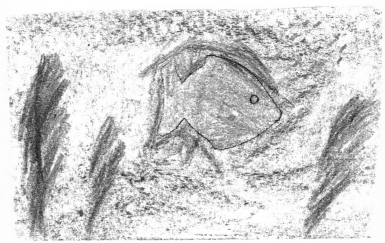

by Emma Higgins
age 7

Oh LORD
Please See Me
through My exams in
two years time as I
need these exams
to get a deb and
please give me a
good life when I
grow up

by *signature*

Lee wolloff
Jon Burrows 4G.

Dial 608 for God

Please God . . . .

- Hello God, you remember me?
- Well, I was ringing to ask if there was any chance I could win a million on the pools, you see I'm a bit broke.
- What would I do with ? Oh!, I'd probably buy a nicer house with a swimming pool and maybe a Jacuzzi, I've always wanted one of those.
- Will it make me a better person? I don't know really it'll make me a nicer one.
- Me, greedy, what! Think of all those millionaires that make bombs and nuclear weapons.
- Do I want to be like them? I guess not. Couldn't I just have half a million? I really need that Jacuzzi.
- Will it make me cleaner inside. I guess not.
- What about a thousand pounds, you can afford that.
- What do you mean, other people need it more than me, like who?
- O.K., O.K., so I'll just have a hundred pounds.
- I know some children haven't got enough to eat or anywhere to live. How about fifty pounds to buy myself a new outfit.
- Some children never have new outfits. I tell you what, I'll get some friends together and raise some money to help children who need food and clothing.
- i'm glad you agree.
- Cheerio!

by Karolina Kennerley (14)
Tracey Price (14)
Jocelyn Anthony (14)

Dear God,

Please can the people in South
Africa get some food ant live
in a healthy country. Thank you
for my mum and dad and for
my warm bed and food. Please
may everybody in the world be
loved.

Amen

by
Vicki
Collings
Age
10

Dear Lord,

Please help my second favourite Football team
to win the triple, Notts Forest. I have
supported them for a number of years and
be grateful if they thrash Liverpool 5.0.

Amen.

Anon

Please God help us

when we are in trouble.

Thank you

Martin Langham age 8 years

Oh, Brother.

Dear God

    Why do people stare at him and think that he's not right. It isn't his fault so why do they make fun of him. He laughs and cries just like us. He cannot talk yet we know what he means. Before he could'nt hear but with all his determination he now hears every word we say. People don't seem to understand that the handicapped people of the world often have more courage and will to do better things in their lives than we have. Please help us all to understand, that when we see someone who is not like us that we should think, and we will find that their not so disserent after all.
    Amen.

By
    Joanne
        Bursnall
    Age 11yrs.

...Stop
the
fighting

God why do we have it.

Nuclear power, bombs etc.

Make them stop.

Stop them now.

Killing the earth and you and me.

Amen.

By Carl Hudson (14) and Ian Vinsen (14)

Dear God

Please Help us to stop all the peopl that sight.
All you hear on the news is that more sighting has started up.
All we ever do is sight and I do not like it so
please help us.

A Men.   Adam Randles 11

NO 'MORE WARS

Dear lord

Please help the sick and
Bereaved and the dying and please help
Me and my mum and dad have a safe
Journey to Greece because we are worried
About the recent air disasters Also help
People to stop fighting around the world
Because they are destroying everything including
Themselves and we don't want a repeat of
The two world wars. In Jesus name we
Pray , Amen

by James King

by James King

Dear
God.

Please will you make
the world safer than it
is now and make there
not be any more wars.
Help the leaders of the
world to be more tolerant
A men.

MAtthew sAndwell
age 11

PRAYER.

Please God, stop all this fighting
   Why did you put people on this earth
   If all they are going to do is fight
Guide them and show them PEACE
     if they stop fighting for just one day
Then they would realise just how
        good to the world peace is
Then they would stop fighting
   and wonder why they carried on
            fighting
   So please please please
      God please put some
         Sense into these people

By Samantha Dennis
    49 Burfield St
       Leicester
       LE4-6AP!
          tqu 14!

Dear God,
    I pray to you God, because
you are the one who will help me
whenever I need you.
        Why must people fight?
    Why must people die when you
want the world to live happily?
Thank-you for my mother God

        Amen

                by Meera Panara

Dear Lord,
    Please stop all the wars
going on in the world.
    Please help us to preserve
what you gave us.
    Please prevent the horror
of nuclear war and speed
up disarmaurment.
    So we may live a long
and enjoyable life.

        Amen.

                Anon.

... help the world

O Lord, please help us. People on the Earth are killing each other. They are cutting down forests and polluting the air. The ozone layer is being attacked by C.F.C's. This is the work of man, and man is destroying your Earth.

O Lord, please help us.

Show us the way to peace, Show us the end of destruction and pollution. Please lord, help us restore the Earth to its beauty.

O Lord, please help us.

'O Lord, our Earth is dying'

by Nilchil Thanki

Dear God

Please look down on the people in Ethopia and Sudan that don't have rain. Please make it rain in the 3rd world So that they can grow their crops and not starve

　　　　　　Please
　　　　　　　Lord.
　　　　　Amen

St. John the Baptist School
　Richard Beatson
　　Age 10

Joni Cook. Age 10.   Saint John The Baptist
                       Primary School.

Dear Lord,
Thank you for the world
and all that is in it.
Help us to look after the
Ozone Layer.
Please stop our mums buying,
Spray Cans and Aerosol Sprays.
     Please Lord,
     Amen.

Dear Lord,

Please help OUR world be better so that couples don't split up because of financial difficulties and so the poorer countries get more out of life than they have been. Help them to have more food, clothes and better medical care, and schooling.

Please help

AMEN

Rachel Holloway
4L

God,
    If only we can perform miracles, I would stop man from being greedy and would make him share all the food out with the starving people all around the world, so that they had enough to last them further than eternity.

I would clean up the pollution and save the poor and dying animals from death.

I would punish the cruel and hateful people who hurt, injure or kill people or animals.

Joanne Crane and
Kim Herbert

I would make the world a
much happier place to
live in, where the world
will run on love and trust.
I know this is not really
possibly but could you
please just help us to
prevent any more of
this happening ever again.
To prevent this we would
need greater leaders who
can direct us along the
right path, and make
us not do the bad that
exsists.
So thank-you lord for all
you have done and I hope
we can make this world
a better place with your
help.

Dear God,
We thank you for your wonderful
world and its animals. We pray
for all the little creatures that are
destroyed every time we cut down
a forest. We are sorry we are
destroying your world and the
ozone layer, and creating a
greenhouse effect. We pray for our
homes and families and clothes.
We ask you to protect us and the
people in the third world.
            For Jesus Christ,   Amen

by
Andrew
Rees
age 10

by Jason Biro
age 11

God our father,
thank you for all the living
things and for the beautiful
countryside around us.
Thankyou for our kind loving
families.
Thankyou for all the people in
the world.

Thankyou for the warm houses we
live in.

Amen.

Damen Nourish   age 10

Swan

wolf

cedar

yellow wagtail

Bear

killer wale

Darren Nounsh

Dear Lord,
I just want to ask you to protect your
children in South Africa.
I especially pray for the children of my
age who the police are detaining.
It must be really hard to be black.
Lord, please protect them.

It would be so frightening to lay down at
night and not know what tomorrow
would bring.
Attacks and cat calls.
Unfairness from the police.
Lord, please protect them.

I can't imagine being locked in a cell
for no reason at all.
Being held without trial
Because I was black.
How would they like to change places?
Lord, please protect them.

Thankyou Lord that our society is different.
A person can walk along without being
insulted.
We have fair trials, and are detained for
good reasons.
Thankyou for protecting us and,
Lord, please protect them.
                              Amen.

                    Lisa Marshall   Age 14

God why do you make people
Suffer, why don't you save the people
in Bangladesh? Please Save the people
from death. If you can't save all of
them at least save some. Give food
to the people who haven't got any and
give them blessing. I could help by
raising money so food can go to
them but i can't do everything to save
them. Some other people will have to
help me to save people all over the
world

by Saurabh   Age: 11

by Carley Clark age 10

God we ask you to help us and our
world problems.
Help the animals and wild life
involved in the Alaskan oil slick.
Help Russian people practice thier
beliefs, with out the fear of
being tortured or killed.
Also help the apartait to be
abolished, and black and white
people to have equal rights.
Farther help us to look after
the wonderful world you have
created.
We leave these problems in your
hands.
Amen.

Marcus V

Dear Lord
    We are told about the crime
and violence every day in
the world but are we strong
enough to cope with the stress
of every day life help us
to survive in the world we
live in.
            Amen

                    Gareth Hunt
                    Douglas Jenkins
                    Jon Burtle

Dear Lord,
Help us all to live and work together
peacefully in the world.
Where people disagree show them the truth.
Where people love give them joy and peace.
Help all the people who are sad, or are
in trouble at this time.
Give them hope and peace so that they
may do your will.
Help all world leaders make the right
decisions, so that the whole world will
live, work, love and worship together.
We ask all of this in the name of your
son Jesus Christ.
                    Amen
                       Stephen Hancock

by Deepak
Agnihotri